HOUGHTON MIFFLIN
Reading
A Legacy of Literacy

Animal Habitats

HOUGHTON MIFFLIN   BOSTON · MORRIS PLAINS, NJ

California   ·   Colorado   ·   Georgia   ·   Illinois   ·   New Jersey   ·   Texas

Design, Art Management and Page Production: Kirchoff/Wohlberg, Inc.

ILLUSTRATION CREDITS
4-21 David Austin-Clar. **22-39** Karen A. Jerome. **40-57** Jean & Mou-sien Tseng.

Printed in U.S.A.

ISBN: 0-618-04392-6

23456789-VH-05 04 03 02 01 00

Animal Habitats

Contents

Dear Butterflies...

by Maryann Dobeck
illustrated by David Austin Clar

Strategy Focus

Can Julia's class find a way to save their butterflies? As you read, **evaluate** how the class solves the problem.

"Class," said Mrs. Evans. "Please show Julia around." Julia was starting her school year a little late. She had just moved to a new home.

Julia pointed to a glass tank. "What are they?" she asked. "They look funny."

"They are monarch butterflies," said Seth.

"They don't *look* like butterflies," said Julia.

Hector said, "Right now, they're called
caterpillars. But soon they will turn into
butterflies."

Each caterpillar had yellow, black, and white stripes.

"Eww!" said Julia. She watched the caterpillars eat the leaves. "Do they eat grass too?"

"No," said Michael. "They only eat milkweed leaves."

"Ugh!" said Julia. "How boring!"

"No, they really like those leaves," Seth laughed.
"It's like having pizza all the time!"

"How do they turn into butterflies?" asked Julia.

"Look," said James. He pointed to the wall.
"We've made a poster that tells you how."

1 In late summer, the monarch butterfly lays her tiny white egg on a milkweed plant.

2 A small caterpillar comes from the egg. Its stripes are pretty.

3 The caterpillar eats the milkweed leaves.

12

4 The caterpillar grows. Its skin falls off. This looks icky!

5 Then the big caterpillar hangs upside down. It wraps itself in a green and gold case.

6 In about two weeks, the case breaks open.

Out comes a monarch butterfly! It is really beautiful!

"Will we keep the butterflies here?" asked Julia.

"No," said Mrs. Evans. "They fly to Mexico to spend the winter where it's warm. But we have a problem."

Mrs. Evans went on. "We just got the caterpillars last week. It's too late in the fall for them to make the trip. They won't find enough food along the way."

"We've been trying to think of ways to help them," said Kim. "So they won't die."

"Maybe we could mail them to Mexico," said Emily.

"We can't put butterflies in the mail," said Kim.

"No," said Julia. "But maybe we can fly them on an airplane. I'll ask my father. He's a pilot."

By the time the caterpillars turned into
butterflies, the class had a plan. They put the
butterflies in a box with tiny holes.

Julia's father came to class on his way to work.
Julia gave him the box.

"I'll be very careful with them," he said. "By the
end of the day, I'll set them free in Mexico."

That night Julia wrote in her journal.

Dear Butterflies,
I hope that you are as
happy in your new home as
I am in mine.

Love,

Julia Rodriguez

Responding

Think About the Selection

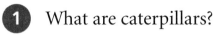

1 What are caterpillars?

2 Find a sentence from the story that tells a fact about the butterfly's diet and another that tells an opinion about it.

Fact and Opinion

Copy the chart on a piece of paper. Read the sentences. They are from the poster in the story. Then tell which sentences are facts and which are opinions.

Statement	Fact	Opinion
A small caterpillar comes from the egg.	✓	
Its stripes are pretty.		✓
The caterpillar grows bigger.	?	?
Its skin falls off.	?	?
This looks icky!	?	?
Out comes a monarch butterfly!	?	?
It is really beautiful!	?	?

Henry and the Fox

by Giovanni De Carlo
illustrated by Karen A. Jerome

Strategy Focus

Who will keep Henry from feeling lonely this summer? Stop every two or three pages to **summarize** what you have read.

Henry lived on a farm. All his school friends lived in town. Now school was out for summer. Henry hoped he would not be too lonely on the farm.

Henry liked to wheel all over the farm.
He fed the chickens. He picked up eggs.
He watched the silverfish in the stream.

Of all the places on the farm, Henry liked the raspberry patch best. He went there every day. One day, something caught his eye. A tiny red fox was standing near him.

Henry sat very still. The fox was trying to eat the
bright, red berries in the bushes. "She looks too
small," thought Henry. "She must be hungry."

Slowly Henry picked one raspberry. He tossed
it to the fox. She ran off before the berry hit the
ground. Henry waited, but the fox didn't
come back.

The next day, the fox *did* come back. Henry
tossed a raspberry again. This time she ate it.
Henry tossed another, and another.

Every day, the fox came back. She ate all the raspberries Henry tossed to her.

"I've made a new friend!" thought Henry.

For three weeks, Henry visited with the
little fox. Then one day she didn't show up.
She didn't come the next day, either.

One day, Henry was wheeling across the farm.
He heard something. It sounded like crying.

Henry followed the sound past the raspberry patch. He followed the sound into the woods. The sound got louder.

Henry saw a wire box. It was a trap. Inside the trap was the little red fox!

She had been making the sound.

The fox saw Henry. She stopped crying. She
came to the door and looked up at him. Henry
leaned down and opened the door.

The fox ran out. She stopped and looked at
Henry as if to say, "Thank you!" Then she ran
into the woods.

Henry didn't see the fox again that summer.

Fall came. The sky got gray. The winds
grew colder.

Soon winter snows covered the raspberry patch.

Spring came again. The skies got blue. The wind got warmer.

At the raspberry patch, something caught Henry's eye.

There was his friend, the fox!

The fox was bigger now. She was not alone.
She had two pups!

Henry grinned as he watched them play. This
summer, he would have *three* fox friends.

Responding

Think About the Selection

1 Where does Henry live?

2 At the beginning of the story, Henry feels he might be too lonely. How does he feel at the end of the story?

Compare and Contrast

Copy the chart on a piece of paper. Mark how Henry and the fox are the same and different.

	Henry	Fox
Likes raspberries.	✓	✓
Was caught in a trap.	?	?
Has a wheelchair.	?	?
Became friends.	?	?

THE UPSIDE-DOWN ELEPHANT

by Yoko Mia Hirano
illustrated by Jean & Mou-sien Tseng

Strategy Focus

What can Nilu do when he finds an elephant that is upside down? **Monitor** your reading to make sure each part of the story makes sense.

Nilu (NEE-loo) looked out at the sun.
He had the whole day to play in the
forest! The forest was his favorite
place. He jumped out of bed.

After breakfast, Nilu walked quickly through his neighborhood. He hoped his little sister wouldn't follow him.

Soon Nilu was at the forest. He looked for
the drawings he had made in the dirt last
week. They were gone. Then he heard a noise.

Had Nilu's little sister come after him? She couldn't have. There was no place for her to hide. Then Nilu saw the big ditch nearby.

Nilu walked to the side of the ditch.
Suddenly he jumped back. There was an
elephant in the ditch! The elephant was
upside down!

The elephant didn't look very happy. Now and then, it moved its big legs in the air.

Nilu ran home to tell his parents.

Soon everybody in the neighborhood knew about the elephant.

Many people went with Nilu back to the ditch. The elephant was still there. It was still upside down.

Uncle Shardul (Shar-**DOOL**) looked worried.
"An elephant needs to stand on its feet or it
will die," he said. "We'll have to pull him out."

"But how?" cried Nilu. No one seemed to know.

Suddenly Mr. Ghatak (Gah-**TACK**) smiled. "I have an idea!" he said. "I'll be back."

Mr. Ghatak came back. He was in a small
truck with a crane and three strong chains.
"Now we can pull the elephant out," he said.

Mr. Ghatak put one of the chains around the elephant. Nilu held his breath as Mr. Ghatak raised the crane.

Snap! The chain broke. Everyone sighed.

"Don't worry," said Mr. Ghatak. "It'll work this time, for sure!" He put another chain around the elephant.

Again, Nilu held his breath.

Snap! The second chain broke. Mr. Ghatak
reached for the third chain.

"That won't work either," thought Nilu.
"We need to try something else."

Nilu jumped into the muddy ditch. He pushed the elephant as hard as he could. Other people jumped in too. Very slowly, they pushed the elephant out.

The elephant stood up. Everybody cheered!

Nilu's sister asked, "Where will the elephant go?"

"Deep into the forest," said Nilu. "We'll take him."

Everybody walked the elephant back to its home. Nilu felt happy.

"I hope we'll see him again," Nilu joked. "Right side up, next time!"

Responding

THINK ABOUT THE SELECTION

1. What does Nilu find in the ditch?

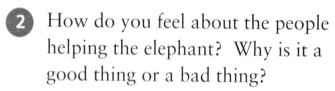

2. How do you feel about the people helping the elephant? Why is it a good thing or a bad thing?

MAKING JUDGMENTS

Copy this chart on a piece of paper. Then complete it to show a judgment you made about Nilu.

What the Character Does	What I Think About It	Why I Think This
Mr. Ghatak brings a crane and chains.	Mr. Ghatak is kind because he wants to help the elephant.	It is a good thing to help animals who are in trouble.
Nilu jumps into the ditch to push the elephant.	?	?